IN THE ARENA

Building the Skills for Peak Performance in Leading Schools and Systems

Dr. Timothy G. Quinn

with
Michelle E. Keith

Quinn and Associates, Ltd.
Old Mission, Michigan

Published by Quinn and Associates, Ltd., PO Box 157, Old
Mission, MI 49673
timquinn@mileader.com

Other titles from this author include:

*The Superintendent Search Process: A Guide to Getting
the Job and Getting Off to a Great Start*

*Peak Performing Governance Teams: Creating an
Effective Board/Superintendent Partnership*

*These titles, and additional copies of this monograph, are
available through major online bookstores.*

**All profits from the sale of this monograph are dedicated to the
continuing development of high needs youth.**

ISBN: 1453865845
EAN-13: 9781453865842

In the Arena

*It is not the critic who counts, not the man who points
how the strong man stumbled or where the doer of
deeds could have done them better.*

*The credit belongs to the man who is actually in the
arena; whose face is marred by dust and sweat and
blood;*

*who strives valiantly; who errs and comes short again
and again;*

*who knows the great enthusiasms, the great devotions,
and spends himself in a worthy cause;*

*who, at the best, knows the triumph of high
achievement;*

*and who, at the worst, if he fails, at least fails while
daring greatly,
 so that his place shall never be with those cold and
timid souls
who know neither victory nor defeat.*

-     *Theodore Roosevelt, 1910*

IN THE ARENA

Building the Skills for Peak Performance in Leading Schools and Systems

Contents   Page

Foreword

There have literally been thousands of books and articles written on the topic of leadership. Some have been based on research studies. Many have focused on the lessons learned by a single leader. Others have focused on the different types of leadership required in different situations, and still others have focused on leadership styles and characteristics.

What I hope to add to the field through this monograph is a practical resource written for and specifically focused on peak performing school leaders, from teacher leaders and coaches through building principals to the superintendency.

Following my retirement from the presidency of a small college at age 50, I was considering starting a consulting business, but knew I wanted my work to continue to focus on public leadership. Over my career, I had observed—and continue to observe—a lack of strong and courageous leadership at all levels of public education, from local schools through higher education. This both concerned and frustrated me, and I began reflecting upon the causes.

Another observation over my career that always befuddled me was the demise of some very good people in public leadership roles. I could cite countless unfortunate examples, but let me provide two that seem fairly representative of patterns of behavior that lead to the demise of leadership careers. These go beyond the well-publicized "acts of stupidity in public"—being caught driving under the influence, being charged with spousal or child abuse, personal misuse of district resources, or other blatant ethics violations.

The first example is a superintendent who was very competent, but was unable or unwilling to assess and effectively manage the politics around a particular issue. Perhaps she had reached a point of frustration that resulted in declaring, "I'm sick and tired of dealing with this (*insert one*) board, union, parent group, etc." When you hear that type of talk from school leaders, the conclusion of their tenure in that role is on the not-too-distant horizon. They, for some reason, have lost their capacity to step back from a situation, take a deep breath, and rethink their approach.

The second example is a principal who lost his courage in the face of conflict and controversy. He began to demonstrate uncertainty and became viewed as weak. His supervisor, board members, and other key constituents stepped into the leadership vacuum, which undermined the principal's credibility and resulted in his departure. This lack of courage plagues many schools and systems and keeps them from fulfilling their mission of outstanding service to children.

As a lifelong student of leadership in its many forms and settings, I decided to find out why some people survive and thrive as great leaders and others do not. Is successful leadership dependent upon genetic traits? Is it dependent upon the personal qualities of the individual? Is it what they do? Or is success determined by the situation they find themselves in?

In pursuit of the answers to these questions, I took most of a full year to immerse myself in the study of leadership, reading what both historic and modern-day gurus have written on the topic, attending leadership seminars, and interviewing respected leaders. Because K-12 education has always been closest to my heart, I focused the application of my findings on school leadership, although the work can be applied to almost any leadership role. These findings were used as the basis for formation of The Michigan Leadership Institute (MLI) in 1999, with a mission of defining, developing and deploying outstanding and inspirational school leaders. Since then, MLI has sponsored numerous leadership development programs, most notably an annual school superintendents preparation academy (SUPES

Academy). Over 500 school leaders have graduated from that program, with approximately 35% becoming superintendents. In addition, MLI has conducted over 150 superintendent searches. (I left MLI in 2009, and its work continues today under the guidance of one of our most gifted and competent associates.)

In 2001, I was engaged by The Broad Center for the Management of School Systems as a partner in the development and implementation of a national academy to train and support superintendents for large, urban districts across the country. The Broad Superintendents Academy started in 2002, and, as of today, has prepared over 130 executive leaders from the education, military, private and non-profit sectors for the superintendency. In these roles, I have enjoyed the opportunity to teach and to advise dozens of superintendents through the superintendent search process, during their entry into the position, and as they have made career transitions.

This monograph also borrows from my reflections on a forty-year career as an English teacher and coach, assistant principal, principal, assistant superintendent, superintendent, deputy state superintendent, and college president.

But my work over the past dozen years has been the most informative to this offering. Through the Leadership Institute and The Broad Center, I have had an incredibly rich opportunity to work with aspiring and established leaders from all walks of life as they've taken on school leadership roles across the country. I've watched school leaders at all levels excel, stumble, fall, and rise again, and—in a few instances—fail dismally. I've learned leadership lessons from each and every one.

In the interest of full disclosure, after reflecting upon my own career, studying the topic of leadership, and observing those I have helped to prepare and mentor, it has become so clear and so very humbling to understand that I was never a *great* leader. Yes, I got things done, and there were those times "in the zone" when I was pretty good—but I was never as great as others I've had the opportunity to observe in action.

If I'd only known then what I know now! There are so many things I'd have done differently had I understood what peak performing leadership was all about. My impact as a leader could have been greater and the organizations I led might have been even stronger upon my departure.

My hope is that this compact and practical monograph will be a useful tool for superintendents, school principals, charter school or private school leaders, lead classroom teachers and coaches. It is a personal leadership workbook that can (and should) be revisited on a periodic basis throughout a career for continuing personal and professional growth. Peak performing leadership evolves over time, and is the result of consistent, conscious reflection, growth, and self-discipline.

In addition, it is my hope that leaders will also be great teachers by sharing this information and discussing it with their teams. Great leaders are needed throughout every school system, at every level. Our children deserve nothing less.

Tim Quinn

Acknowledgements

At the conclusion of this monograph, there is a list of additional suggested readings on the topic of leadership. These are some of the best writings on this topic and represent those authors and leaders who have most influenced my thinking. I want to thank all of them for their contributions to the field and apologize in advance if my limited capacity to comprehend their message has misrepresented their viewpoint in any way.

I would also like to thank all of the great leaders, mentors, and coaches I've met along the way. The opportunity to observe them both up close and from afar—at their very best and sometimes when they've been something less than they aspired to be—has provided the richest learning experience of my career. Their work is reflected in this writing.

Thanks also to my editor, John Bebow, for his work in helping me with this writing. It must have been akin to making a silk purse out of a sow's ear.

Several "critical friends" reviewed an early version of this monograph and offered their much-appreciated and very astute observations, stories, and advice. I respect each and every one of them as a great educational leader. Thanks to John Barry, Barbara Byrd-Bennett, Tom Brady, Ray Cortines, Maria Goodloe-Johnson, Pete Gorman, Mike Hill, Melody Johnson, Dan Katzir, Becca Bracy Knight, Dan Pappas, Tom Payzant, Tom Pridgeon, Mark Roosevelt, John Simpson, and Michael Wilmot for their feedback.

And, most importantly, I'd like to acknowledge my life partner, co-conspirator and co-author on this project, Shelley Keith, who is able to take great and diverse random thoughts, put them together, and make sense out of them.

Dedication

This book is dedicated to our nation's 50+ million school-age children—all of whom will need a high quality education in order to survive and thrive in the world they will inhabit as adults.

It is especially dedicated to those among them who are trapped in schools and systems where the adults either do not have the capacity—or the will—to make the changes needed to ensure a high quality education for all children. These are the kids without voice and without agency who are waiting for great leaders to step up on their behalf and save them from a slow but certain demise. These great leaders must provide the opportunity for <u>all</u> children to develop their full potential and have the full and vibrant life that only comes with a high-quality education.

From a Child in a Failing School
To All School Leaders

Whisper in My Heart

So it tells me that you're coming,
This whisper in my heart.
It tells me that you're coming
To take this place apart.

So it tells me that you're brave,
It tells me that you're smart.
It tells me you'll be strong,
This whisper in my heart.

So it tells me I deserve you
That I, too, am smart and strong.
It tells me that you'll save me
As these whispers rise to song.

So it tells me that you're coming
To save me from this fate.
I hope that you will hurry—
I pray you're not too late!

Introduction

Schools today need great leadership, at all levels of the organization.

I firmly believe that the education of our children is the critical key to America's future. Today—in all too many states, in all too many systems, and in all too many schools—we are short-changing our children and grandchildren by giving them a preparation to live in a global economy that is inferior to the preparation received by children in other countries. *America is no longer even among the top 20 countries on any international measure of student achievement.* The only measure we rank among the highest is in terms of inequality—having the 4th largest performance gap between high- and low-socioeconomic status children. (2006 PISA results, OECD) **This is completely and unequivocally unacceptable if our nation is to survive and thrive.** Across the country—in urban, suburban, and rural districts alike—our schools can do better, all the adults can do better, and we can expect more from all children.

At the same time, I firmly believe that *leadership* is the key ingredient in the success or failure of any organization, schools and school systems included.

School systems are often the largest organizations in their communities, having the greatest number of employees and the biggest budgets. Some larger school districts may have more employees and bigger budgets than any other entity in their entire state. In fact, a number of school systems are as large as some of the biggest corporations in America. The New York City Department of Education, for example, would rank among the top of the Fortune 500 list in terms of size, with its budget of over $20 billion and its 80,000+ employees.

In addition to the normal challenges of running a human-intensive, complex organization, school leaders often face the special challenges of low student achievement, high dropout rates, dysfunctional operating systems, difficult boards, facilities in urgent need of repair, tricky labor issues, and funding that doesn't begin to keep up with costs—just to name a few. School leaders seeking to overcome those challenges also often operate within a highly political, racially-sensitive, media-intensive, bureaucratic, and highly regulated public environment. The fact that schools are most often the biggest spenders of local taxpayer dollars and are charged with the care and development of a community's most precious resource—its children—places everything school leaders do under the community's magnifying glass. **School leaders are truly "in the arena."**

In spite of all these challenges, I will repeat that I firmly believe *effective leadership* is the key ingredient in the success or failure of any school or system. Not more money, not different labor laws, not different politics, not new programs. *Great leadership—both inside and outside the classroom—is the only "Silver Bullet."*

While other leadership roles in both the public and private sectors can be demanding, no job is as challenging as that of the school leader—when done right. And, when done right, **no job is more rewarding**.

> *There comes a special moment in everyone's life, a moment for which that person was born. That special opportunity, when he seizes, will fulfill his mission – a mission for which he is uniquely qualified. In that moment he finds greatness. It is his finest hour.*
> *(Sir Winston Churchill)*

Given this environment, to be successful as a school leader, **you need to fully understand who you are as a leader, what you believe, and why you are doing this work.** You must be completely confident and comfortable in your own skin. You must have the courage of your beliefs and convictions in order to stand up to the often relentless pressures of competing interests—interests that are at times in conflict with the best interests of children.

And, you must wake up each and every day knowing in your heart that you have been "called" to this mission.

This monograph is not about the technical side of managing a school or school system. Rather, it is primarily about YOU—you as a leader and the interpersonal and intrapersonal skills necessary to become a great school leader. Some refer to these skills as the "soft skills" of leadership. But it has been my observation that these soft skills represent the dimensions of leadership that are the most essential to success—and that most leaders have the most difficulty mastering.

As others have noted, *"The soft stuff is truly the hard stuff."*

I'm going to begin our conversation by defining leadership in this context. Then I will discuss the qualities and characteristics of the most effective school leaders I have had the opportunity to observe. For the sake of clarity, I have labeled these the "Characteristics of Peak Performing School Leaders." However, the characteristics apply to leaders at all levels of a district—from lead teacher to principal to superintendent, and everyone in between.

The Leadership Workbook section of this monograph provides many practical exercises for helping you put the characteristics into action in your own practice of leadership.

Additional resources are shared in the Appendices, including an outline for a corresponding book study discussion with your own leadership team.

Defining Leadership

In my readings, I've found countless descriptions of great leaders and their qualities, characteristics and skills. There are almost as many definitions of leadership as there have been great leaders and scholars who have observed and studied them. I've concluded that leadership—and especially school leadership—is as complex as life itself. There are always more questions than answers.

What's critical is for anyone who takes on a leadership role to keep reflecting upon and honing their own definition of leadership, their own leadership philosophies, and their own leadership skills. The leader is never "finished" with the tasks of leadership definition and personal leadership development. It is a lifelong routine that should conclude only when you draw your final breath.

By the time you finish this book, it is my hope that you will have defined leadership in your own terms, knowing full well that your definition will change over time as you grow and evolve as a leader.

The point is, if you are going to be a peak performing leader, you need to be able to define leadership in your own terms because as the "first teacher" in the organization, you will need to teach others to lead as well. The days are long gone when a single individual could be a "lone ranger" leader, at any level of the system. The work is too important, too complex, and too great for one person to master alone.

So let's consider what some of the great thought leaders have said about this topic over the years. The very first reference I found about leadership comes from the Chinese philosopher Lao Tzu, in the 6th century BC. He said:

To lead people, walk beside them.
True leaders are hardly known to their followers.
Next after them are the leaders the people honor and
praise;
After them, those they fear;
After them, those they despise.
When the best leader's work is done
The people say, "We did it ourselves!"

The essence of Lao Tzu's definition of leadership is reflected in what Jim Collins, in his book *Good to Great*, calls "Level 5 Leadership." He identified five levels of leaders:

- **Level 1** leaders are *highly capable individuals* who make productive contributions through their talent and hard work
- **Level 2** leaders are *contributing team members* who contribute to the achievement of group objectives and work well with others
- **Level 3** leaders are *competent managers* who organize people and resources in pursuit of predetermined objectives
- **Level 4** leaders are *effective leaders*, who lead a group to high performance in pursuit of a clear, compelling vision
- **Level 5 *executive leaders* build enduring greatness through humility and resolve, also known as professional will.**

Humility will be a consistent theme throughout this writing. While having a strong and healthy ego is important in a leadership role, keeping it in check is even more important. Being able to set your ego aside for the benefit of the organization and those it serves is absolutely critical to becoming a Lao Tzu "True Leader," a

It's hard to imagine a Level 5 leader thinking, "Hey, that Rambo character reminds me of me."
(Jim Collins)

Collins "Level 5 Leader," or what we call a **Peak Performing School Leader.**

A few other leadership definitions worthy of note:

From the Center for Creative Leadership,
> *"Leadership is a process, not a position."*

From John Gardner,
> *"Leadership is both a science and an art; it is rational and emotional."*

From Jay Conger, in his book *Spirit at Work,*
> *"A leader is someone who has the extraordinary power to project onto other people his or her darkness or light."*

Robert Greenleaf, founder of the Greenleaf Center for Servant Leadership, states,
> *"Leadership is the ability to state a goal and reach it, through the efforts of other people, and satisfy those whose judgment one respects, under conditions of stress."*

And from Charles Kiefer,
> *"Leadership is what we call it when we see someone doing something they love and we want to help."*

One of my favorite definitions, author unknown, is,
> *"Leadership is the inability to stand around with your hands in your pockets and watch something you care about fall apart."*

One definition I've developed and used for a number of years is,
> *"Leadership is serving as a catalyst for the movement of people from where they are to a significantly better place."*

One superintendent recently spoke to a group of 150 seventh graders attending a leadership conference. She asked them the difference between a manager/boss and a leader. One incredible child answered:

> *"People do what a boss says because they have to. But they do what a leader says because they want to."*

As noted above, there are hundreds, if not thousands, of definitions of leadership, and rightly so. **All leaders need to define leadership on their own terms, expressing what it means to them. They need to use that definition as the basis for their leadership practice and as the basis for teaching others to lead.**

How do *you* define leadership? What does being a leader mean to you? Drafting a working definition is just the first step. Living it and teaching it to others allows you to put it to the test and make it better.

Putting It into Practice

Complete **ASSIGNMENT 1: "DEFINING LEADERSHIP,"** found on page 65 of the *Leadership Work Book* section of this monograph.

Characteristics of Peak Performing School Leaders

Now let's talk about the qualities, skills, and characteristics of what we call Peak Performing School Leaders. *(Please note that these characteristics apply to all levels of school leadership—from lead teacher to superintendent. For the sake of clarity, I simply refer to "school leadership" throughout.)*

Again, the literature is full of lists of leadership skills, characteristics and behaviors. I've narrowed these down to the ten I have observed to be the most important for highly effective and successful school leadership. Perhaps I should first explain what I consider "highly effective and successful school leadership." I define this by two criteria:

1) being able to significantly improve student achievement and close achievement gaps, and
2) being able to manage all the other aspects of the job in a manner that allows you to stay on the job long enough to accomplish #1.

These characteristics of Peak Performing School Leaders are not listed in any particular order of importance. They are all intertwined and, in most instances, interdependent.

I believe that Peak Performing School Leaders:
1. Have received and responded to the calling of leadership
2. Have a coherent and comprehensive belief system
3. Are dedicated masters of self
4. Are dedicated servants of others
5. Are enthusiastic and passionate about their work and are authentic human beings
6. Assume the role of first learner, first teacher, first advocate, and first collaborator on behalf of children

7. Are visionary, define success in measurable terms, and have a strategy for achieving success
8. Are politically astute
9. Are trustworthy and competent
10. Have the courage to lead deep

Each of these characteristics will be discussed in depth, and corresponding exercises in the Leadership Workbook section of this monograph will help the reader develop his or her own leadership skills.

1. Peak Performing School Leaders have received and responded to the calling of leadership.

Peak Performing School Leaders have answered the questions: Who am I? What is my purpose? What is my personal vision? What are my strengths? My values, key intelligences, and passions? How am I going to make a contribution to the greater good of human kind? When all is said and done, what difference will my life have made?

Finding your "calling" comes out of that ongoing conversation we have with ourselves about how this life is going—that periodic "taking stock" of our lives, and then acting on that information with passion, discipline, and resolve.

Philosopher Frederick Buechner says that your particular *calling*, or *vocation, is the one in which your deep gladness and the world's deep need meet—something that not only makes you happy but that the world needs to have done.*

This is a "knowing" of who you are, what your life is about, what it is you get up to do every single day, and why.

This is the true joy in life—being used for a purpose recognized by yourself as a mighty one.
(George Bernard Shaw)

Having a calling provides leaders with a certainty about the direction they must pursue. It is a fundamental self-knowledge. It provides an ever-present internal compass that won't be ignored.

Pursuing a calling can be challenging, difficult, and downright scary. But pursuing your greatest passion puts you in a position where you automatically attract followers—people will, as Kiefer suggested, see you doing something you love and they will want to help. Mahatma

Gandhi, the most notable founder of the non-violent movement, spoke of this when discussing leadership. He stated, "When you pursue your greatest passions, you'll be amazed at who you'll find by your side." His life embodied that belief, and he had no shortage of followers by his side when he chose to pursue his life's purpose, even when marching into the most dangerous of circumstances.

Rudyard Kipling wrote of the concept of a calling in his poem *The Explorer* (1898). Here are a few excerpts:

There's no sense in going further
So they said, and I believed it – broke my land and sowed my crop –
Built my barns and strung my fences in the little border station
Tucked away below the foothills where the trails run out and stop.

Till a voice, as bad as conscience, rang interminable changes
On one everlasting Whisper day and night repeated – so:
"Something hidden. Go and find it. Go and look behind the Ranges –
Something lost behind the Ranges. Lost in waiting for you. Go!"

Over the next 18 stanzas of that poem, Kipling tells the story, through the eyes and voice of his explorer, of the incredible hardships endured because he chose to respond to that calling. **But,** he also talks about the incredible discoveries his explorer made—the vast plains, beautiful lakes, rivers, and mountain ranges, and how he staked out markers for others to follow. In the final stanza, Kipling's explorer sits listening to others who had followed his markers, and who are telling the story of "their" great discoveries. In the final line, Kipling's explorer refutes those story tellers. He says, *"No these were not their great discoveries, nor were they mine. These were God's great* *gift to our great nation, but,"* he said, *"the Whisper came to me."*

So, one of the great challenges and responsibilities of a leader is to answer the question: "What is whispering to me?" And, "How am I going to respond to this whisper?"

Great leaders believe they have been placed here for a purpose—an opportunity to take the gifts they've been given and use them to make a difference in the lives of others. There is no opportunity for making a greater mark on the world than serving as a school leader. Every person in this role should feel that they have been "called" to leadership on behalf of our children—our future.

Many great school leaders love working directly with children in the classroom and are sometimes reluctant to move into a different leadership role. In our work, we have interviewed hundreds of school leaders and always like to ask how and why they felt "called" to school leadership. Here are the typical responses:

- They wanted to make an impact at a broader level and contribute to a greater good.
- A mentor saw their potential and encouraged them.
- They felt they could do a better job than others they observed in a district leadership role.
- A family member influenced them to assume greater challenges.
- They wanted to progress in their career, and were afraid of ending up like the 30-year staff veterans who had quit growing.
- They were responding to a spiritual need to do more.

A couple of caveats here—first, in viewing your leadership role as a "calling," don't make the mistake of concluding that those who may oppose you don't have a valid perspective worthy of your consideration. Arrogance can be a leader's worst enemy. More than one school leader has taken the position that, "I'm here to serve the interests of children, and I don't have the time or the patience to deal with the interests of adults." They failed to remember that as a school leader, while you are primarily responsible for meeting the needs of students, you cannot ignore or disregard the interests of others who are part of the teaching and learning equation.

Second, although those choosing educational leadership are often pursuing their calling through their work, it's important to recognize that not everyone is able to do this. Some people, simply due to economics or life circumstances, have to pursue their calling through their avocation outside of work life. These people may end up being some of your school's best parent or community volunteers.

Putting It into Practice

To begin reflection on your calling, complete Step 1 of **ASSIGNMENT 2: "PERSONAL LEADERSHIP PLAN,"** found on page 67 of the *Leadership Work Book* section of this monograph.

---

2. Peak Performing School Leaders have a coherent and comprehensive belief system.

Great leaders are knowledgeable, and—based upon the knowledge they've developed through continuous study, experience, observation, and reflection—they establish beliefs. They know what they believe:

- About themselves in the context of their leadership role
- About children and their capacity to achieve
- About the role of schools
- About leadership teams
- About the role of principals
- About effective governance
- About the role of teachers
- About the role of parents
- About the role of the community in supporting its children

Your beliefs are the basis for your day-to-day decision-making. These beliefs will evolve over time with new knowledge and experiences.

Don't place yourself in a position of responsibility for a team, classroom, school, or an entire system and the lives of a community's children without

You'll see it when you believe it.
(DeWitt Jones)

having your comprehensive belief system in order. Thinking about all of this on the fly during the interview process or in the heat of the moment on the job is far too late, plus it will quickly get "sniffed out" by your staff and your rivals once you're on the job.

Remember, if you don't know what you believe, or if you can't clearly articulate those beliefs, those you would have as followers will never believe in you.

I recall very clearly the example of a very bright, charismatic and articulate district administrator who got through a private, fast-tracked interview process for a superintendency with surprising ease. Unfortunately, he was also a bit intellectually lazy, a bit disorganized, and usually able to convince others to "do" for him. He hadn't taken the time to figure out exactly what it was that he truly believed about kids, public school leadership, or any of the various constituent groups. Almost immediately, his new superintendency was being pecked apart by his leadership team, his board, and his staff. His tenure—eight months.

In his compelling book Leading Minds, Howard Gardner stated that the arena in which leadership occurs is the human mind. Leaders are persons who, by word and/or personal example, markedly influence the behaviors, thoughts, and/or feelings of their followers. In his work with the theory of Multiple Intelligences, Gardner found that three of the eight intelligences are critical for leaders:
1) the intrapersonal—having a deep understanding of self; being self-reflective
2) the interpersonal—interacting well with others; sensitivity to others' needs
3) the verbal-linguistic—being good with the spoken and written word; skilled at explaining, teaching, telling stories, persuasive speaking

Gardner tells us that leaders have to be effective story tellers. They have to be able to tell three stories particularly well. First, they must be able to tell their own story—who they are, key learnings, and experiences that brought them to this point in their leadership journey. We refer to this as their Leadership Story. (See Assignment 4 in the Leadership Workbook section.)

Second, leaders must be able to tell the story of the organization they lead—past, present and future. That is, the history of the organization, its current status in the context of

21. If a course has more than one teacher throughout the school year, how should the teachers be reported? For example: when teacher is out on extended leave, or a teacher taking over a class mid-year.

The system will allow up to three teachers to be associated with a course. It is a local decision as to which teachers to include. If a teacher is responsible for the instruction of a course for a period of time determined to be a significant factor in student growth for the course, he or she should be reported. This may be a teacher (substitute) who is filling in for the teacher-of-record for an extended period of time or a teacher who has taken over as the teacher-of-record for the course. When the growth data is returned, the district must determine how the growth data for the students in that course impact the teachers' effectiveness labels.

22. Do we report substitute teachers?

Substitute teachers should only be reported in the TSDL Collection when they are the teacher of record; i.e., when they assign the student's grade or make grade placement and completion status decisions. In all other cases, reporting a substitute teacher with a course is at the district's discretion.

23. What if two or more teachers are teaching the same course, such as team teaching or co-teaching?

The teacher responsible for student outcomes should be reported. The MSDS allows up to three teachers to be associated with each course for a student. It is a local decision as to which teacher(s) will be held accountable for a student's performance in a particular course. This is applicable for long-term substitute teachers as well. Co-teachers should be able to teach well together. Student

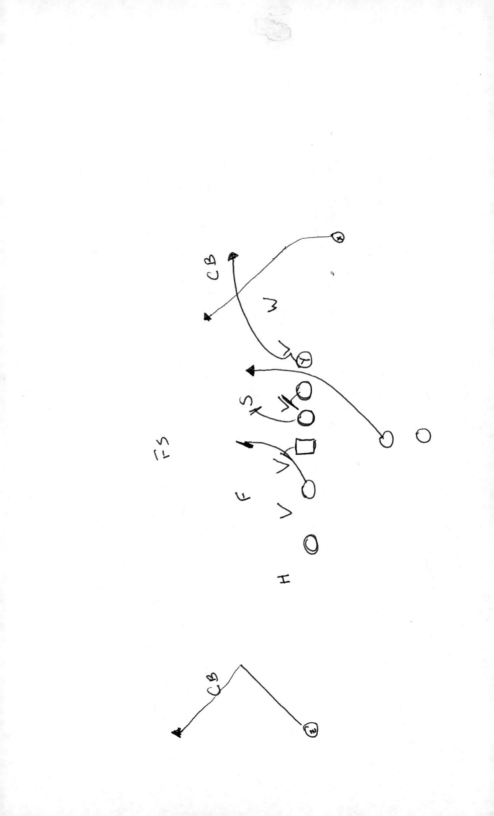

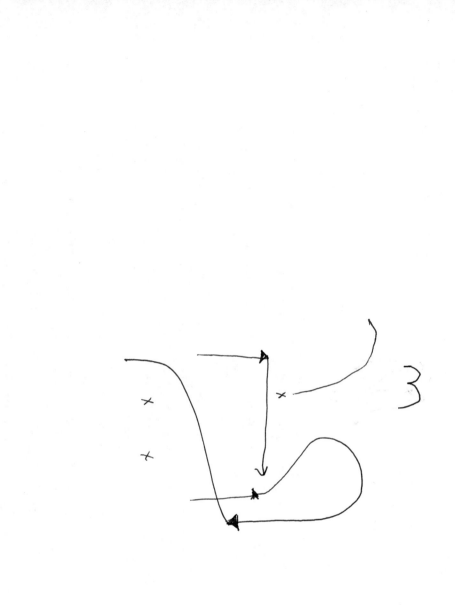

24. Many of our courses are co-taught with special education teachers. Are both considered the teacher of record? How would MSDS handle this?

If it is considered a team-teaching situation, both teachers should be reported. If the special education teachers are providing supplementary assistance and are not considered the teachers of record, it is a local decision to report them. You can report up to three individual teachers per course.

25. If a class is reported as being a virtual class, is it mandatory to report the mentor teacher as the teacher of record or is it optional?

A teacher of record must be reported with the student. If the course is virtual and there is no "teacher of record," then the mentor teacher must be reported. You may indicate that the teacher is working in a mentor capacity rather than as the teacher of record for these virtual instruction situations. A mentor teacher must be a certificated teacher.

26. How do we report online courses or credit recovery courses, (such as compass and/or Michigan Virtual High School), where a local teacher only monitors the students?

Online courses may be reported as Virtual Delivery and the teacher may be identified as a mentor teacher. Credit recovery courses are treated as any other course. If they are being completed through a the community and clients, and their vision for where it needs to go next.

And finally, they must tell the story of the followers and their roles in the context of that vision for the future.

The point is that all of these stories are laden with your beliefs. These beliefs will change over time with continuous learning and observation of what works and what doesn't in various contexts. Taking the time for periodic reflection and the recalibration of your belief system is an important component of your learning. Key words: learning, observation, reflection, recalibration, self-discipline.

We have included a few sample sets of beliefs in Appendix A. This is just a sampling. Make sure you have your own beliefs in place before you assume a leadership role.

Putting It into Practice

Complete **ASSIGNMENT 3: "STATEMENTS OF BELIEF,"** found on page 77 of the *Leadership Work Book* section of this monograph.

Complete **ASSIGNMENT 4: "YOUR LEADERSHIP STORY,"** found on page 79 of the *Leadership Work Book* section of this monograph.

---

3. Peak Performing School Leaders are dedicated masters of self.

When I talk about self-mastery, I'm simply talking about being the very best human being and the very best leader that you can possibly be. I have observed that **people (and leaders) are at their very best when they are growing or helping others grow.** I have also observed that **being a great person is a prerequisite for being a great leader.**

Because the school leader is the first learner and the first teacher in the organization, you need to understand that everything you do is an act of teaching. People are observing you, watching your every move, listening to what you say, noting your behavior, and observing how you handle various situations that arise. **There is nothing you can say that will be more powerful than the lesson of your actions.** All that you do will model the tone and create the culture for the entire organization.

A number of leadership development organizations and gurus talk about what we call personal mastery in the context of the four dimensions of one's life—the **physical**, the **social/emotional**, the **intellectual**, and the **spiritual** dimensions.

When you systematically determine where you are and where you'd like to be in each dimension, and then manage the daily, weekly, monthly and annual activities of your life to support those ends, it leads to mastery—becoming the best possible You. The children within your schools and the people on your staff serving those children deserve your best. **You'll never see or**

> *There's a difference between interest and commitment. When you're interested in doing something, you do it only when circumstances permit. When you're committed to something, you accept no excuses, only results.*
> *(Anonymous)*

believe in *their* full potential unless you are consciously striving to meet your own full potential.

There is an old Native American proverb that states every person is a house with four rooms—the intellectual, the spiritual, the emotional, the physical. It goes on to say that to be whole, to live a full life, you must live in each of your rooms every day. Gandhi also tells us *if you have a problem in one part of your life, you will have a problem in your whole life. If you choose to ignore the problem, it doesn't go away—it only comes back later, in some uglier form that you will eventually have to address.*

With all the important demands of the job, however, many school leaders don't prioritize their own needs very highly. The noted writer and teacher Parker Palmer reminds us that it is not a selfish act to take good care of one's self—that self you were placed on earth to share with others. This is your gift—the gift to you from your Creator that you have a responsibility to develop to its fullest potential. *You must be the diligent keeper of your own temple.*

As we talk about self mastery, let's be mindful that human beings have a natural tendency to be lazy and succumb to inertia. *Discipline* is the key word in self-mastery—exercising control over your own life and taking a systematic approach to your own improvement. Steven Covey talks about exercising influence over the things we can control. Obviously for school leaders, one of the few things you can truly control is yourself.

Let's talk about seeking mastery in each of the four dimensions of your life.

The Physical Dimension. Most of us have known people who died before their time because they didn't take care of themselves. As leaders, maintaining physical health is also important for personal presence, for managing stress and for endurance. During the 18th hour of your day, a problem will

---

inevitably appear on your doorstep. And that problem is usually in the form of another human being who needs your help. The question is: Will you have the personal sense of presence and stamina to be there for them? Can you bring your best self to the needs of the situation?

Your responsibility is to model physical health and life balance. What is your blood pressure? Cholesterol level? Body fat? Do you exercise regularly? Are you eating a healthy diet? Do you have dependency issues? Are you taking care of yourself for the ones who depend upon you professionally and (even more importantly) for those who love you and depend upon you personally? If you are not, you need to get started—it's part of mastery and part of being a great leader.

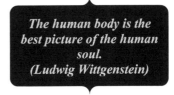

The human body is the best picture of the human soul.
(Ludwig Wittgenstein)

One quick story illustrates this point well. A school superintendent speaking at one of our leadership academies told of a lesson he learned the hard way. He was a hard-charging Type A personality, working sixteen hours a day and thinking he was doing a great service to his system and a great job of supporting his family. Then he had "the big one" right there in his office on a Monday afternoon while prepping for a board meeting. He spent the next 10 days in intensive care. Under doctor's orders, he began daily therapy to help repair his damaged heart. Not long after, he was allowed to return to work on a limited schedule, but with continued daily physical therapy that lasted for a full year. On the first anniversary of "the event," his doctor told him that he was doing well, and that he was no longer required to attend daily physical therapy. This superintendent shared that now, three years since his near-tragedy, he still keeps one hour blocked out for himself each and every day for "therapy." A difficult lesson…one he was grateful to have survived.

The Social/Emotional Dimension. I used to say that leadership was all about the people. While that may be true, I've refined it to say that leadership is all about the *relationships*. It is all about building trusting and lasting relationships that extend far beyond your tenure. When all is said and done, people will not necessarily remember you for what you've accomplished. They'll remember you for what you meant to them, the impact you had on their lives for better or for worse, and the contribution you made to the development of other people along the way.

> *The quality of your life is the quality of your relationships.*
> *(Anthony Robbins)*

The late John Wooden, the fabled UCLA basketball coach, made this point very clearly in his last book A Game Plan for Life: The Power of Mentoring. In this book he reflects, at age 99, upon an incredible career with ten national championships and the receipt of every conceivable award that one could win in his profession. But his reflections barely mention any of those. Rather, he dedicates the entire book to reflecting on the mentoring relationships he enjoyed throughout his life—from his own father, to a special coach, a number of his players, and historical figures whose biographies he found particularly compelling. In his mind, his life's purpose was not about national championships, number of victories, or awards, but all about relationships. That perspective helped make him the most successful college basketball coach of all time—and a great model for leaders everywhere.

If you've gone through a Covey Seven Habits training program, you know that one of the self-exploratory exercises is to envision your 85th birthday party. Who would you want to be there? What testimonials would they share about you and your life? If you take the time to answer those two simple questions and the answers leave you cold, take heart. There is time to change this—unless, of course, you're 85.

We all have heard and read the accounts of 9/11. When the people on those doomed planes understood what was happening, and made their final phone calls, few called in to see how things were going at the office. Rather, they called the people they loved and cared about, the ones most important to them. As a leader, if you are going to be a self master, you must make those relationships a priority and take care of those relationships *first*. They will serve as a foundation for the relationships you need at work to create an organization that is healthy, constructive, and optimal for children. Having solid, grounding relationships with significant others can be a life-saver for a leader.

The Intellectual Dimension. All too often, school leaders assume that because they've achieved the pinnacle of their career, they no longer need to be learners. Nothing could be further from the truth. This is the time when leaders need to grow the most. **If you aren't learning, you aren't leading.** One principal recommends looking forward, not backward— imagine that you can look into the future, and find yourself faced with an incredibly challenging problem. What should you be reading today in order to be able to handle this problem? What should you be studying?

Who is included in your network of professional peers and mentors? Any time leaders move up, they need to reestablish and expand their peer network. It doesn't mean they give up old relationships. But they need to create a new set of peers they can talk to—people who will be most capable of helping with the challenges of the new role. And those peers should be the best leaders you can identify.

Who are your mentors now? Who are you mentoring? Are you teaching on a regular basis? Helping others grow is a great way to keep yourself fresh and growing. *Remember, we're all at our best as human beings when we're growing or helping others grow. We're at our very best when we're doing both.*

The Spiritual Dimension. As I began my research on the topic of leadership, this was one area that I found most stunning. Having served in public institutions for my full career, I hadn't thought much about the spirit as it relates to work. But what I learned from practitioners is that this has nothing to do with the separation of church and state. The vast majority of leaders I interviewed said there was a deeply spiritual dimension to their work.

When talking about spirit, they were not talking about anyone's religion or church. They were talking about a life force that exists in each and every one of us—the spirit that gives us the strength and power to accomplish well beyond what we thought

> *There are some people who have the quality of richness and joy in them and they communicate it to everything they touch. It is first of all a physical quality; then it is a quality of the spirit.*
> *(Thomas Wolfe)*

possible. It is the spirit that connects us to something bigger than ourselves. When we look back on our major accomplishments in life, there was a driving spirit that gave us the capacity to achieve those things. What are you doing to nurture and develop that spirit?

This goes back to the issue of your calling. It is all about making sure our lives are in balance and in alignment with what it is we believe our purpose to be.

Therefore, this becomes a very personal discussion with yourself. Taking time alone for meditation and reflection is critical. The French philosopher Blaise Pascal once said that, "All of man's problems are derived from his inability to spend time in a room alone." If he were alive today, he would have added, "without any electronic devices."

In the whole area of self-mastery, the important thing is for each leader to determine where they are in each dimension of their lives, where they would like to be, develop strategies to get there, and then follow those strategies in a systematic, disciplined manner.

As we become better people, through self mastery, we increase our leadership capacity exponentially.

Putting It into Practice

To begin your work on self-mastery, complete **ASSIGNMENT 2: "PERSONAL LEADERSHIP PLAN,"** found on page 67 of the *Leadership Work Book* section of this monograph.

---

4. Peak Performing School Leaders are dedicated servants of others.

The phrase "Servant Leadership" was coined by Robert K. Greenleaf in *The Servant as Leader,* an essay he first published in 1970. In that essay, he said:

> *"The servant-leader is servant first...It begins with the natural feeling that one wants to serve, to serve first. Then conscious choice brings one to aspire to lead. That person is sharply different from one who is leader first, perhaps because of the need to assuage an unusual power drive or to acquire material possessions... The leader-first and the servant-first are two extreme types. The difference manifests itself in the care taken by the servant-first to make sure that other people's highest priority needs are being served. The best test, and difficult to administer, is: Do those served grow as persons? Do they, while being served, become healthier, wiser, freer, more autonomous, more likely themselves to become servants? And, what is the effect on the least privileged in society? Will they benefit or at least not be further deprived?"*
> *(www.greenleaf.org)*

People don't follow people they don't trust. And they don't trust people they believe are there to serve themselves before serving the clients of the organization, or those who labor day in and day out on the clients' behalf. If you are a school leader primarily for your own purposes—for personal recognition, perhaps to build your resume, your income or your retirement fund—your would-be followers will know that in due time. And when they do, they will not trust you. You won't be leading—you'll simply be out for a walk all by yourself. As soon as you find yourself in a difficult situation, you'll turn around and find no one there to support you.

Being a servant leader also serves *your* highest needs. Most of us learned in Psych 101 about Abraham Maslow, who researched the topic of human motivation. Maslow's basic theory suggests we are all motivated toward the fulfillment of our own needs, and those needs are met in hierarchical order from the physiological, to the safety, love and belongingness, self-esteem and self-actualization needs. But in his final book, *The Further Reaches of Human Nature*, he talked about a higher need—the need he described as transcendence. At the highest levels of human existence, we are motivated to simply serve the needs of other people and to support the growth and fulfillment of others.

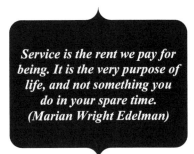

Service is the rent we pay for being. It is the very purpose of life, and not something you do in your spare time. (Marian Wright Edelman)

That's what being a servant leader is all about—living at the highest level of human existence (from a psychological standpoint) by making sure that everybody within the organization is growing, and to the greatest extent possible, creating a situation where the needs of the children and the needs of the adults are being met simultaneously.

I'd like to share an example of a deficit of this characteristic. More than once, I've come across candidates in superintendent searches who have moved up rapidly in their careers—two, specifically come to mind. These bright, articulate, young men had both moved quickly from teacher, to assistant principal, to principal, to central office—often spending only a year or two in each role. Upon getting to know these gentlemen, it became apparent that their motivation for moving up was to achieve greater status, greater salary, and greater benefits. They didn't talk much about what they had done (or could do) for the children.

These up-and-comers had not spent a long enough period of time in any position to learn their leadership lessons and live with some of their leadership mistakes. When they reached the level of the superintendency, they quickly "flamed out." They got caught up in the perks of the job, no longer placed their own phone calls, and worried more about their own contract than about what was happening for kids in the district. People in each organization quickly recognized that their leader was out to serve himself rather than them, and therefore didn't share their trust or their loyalty. These men had so much talent and potential, but they didn't develop an understanding of their real purpose as leaders.

Putting It into Practice

Review what you drafted for **ASSIGNMENT 4: "YOUR LEADERSHIP STORY,"** found on page 79 of the *Leadership Work Book* section of this monograph. Is *service to others* a key theme or core value for you?

***5. Peak Performing School Leaders are enthusiastic and
passionate about their work and are authentic human
beings.***

The word *enthusiasm* is rooted in the Greek language,
meaning *in the spirit*. We know it is something caught, not
taught. We've all observed people lost in their calling,
dancing to the song of their souls. And we've also observed
people who are passionless—who don't seem to care about
what they are doing, are clock watchers, and know the exact
number of years/months/days until retirement.

The question is: Who do you want teaching your children?
Who would you want as principals of the schools your
children attend? The answer is simple: We know who we
want to be in contact with our children at every single turn—
the ones who are enthusiastic and passionate about their
work. And guess what—this passion starts at the top of the
organization—in your heart, in your gut, in your soul. It
begins with the leader.

I once heard the poet and consultant David Whyte cite his
work with troubled organizations. As he tells it, he's usually
invited into organizations needing a turnaround—the ones
failing, in a tailspin, and ready to crash and burn unless
something changes their trajectory. He goes into these
organizations with the pre-condition that he gets to spend
considerable time in the organization before talking with
anyone from the executive staff. Whyte says that in a
relatively brief period of time, he inevitably comes to the
conclusion that he is in what he refers to as a "Lazarus
organization." He defines a Lazarus organization as one
where the people come alive at the end of the day, when they
are leaving the building. They don't bring their spirit to
work—they check it at the door. It is a place where leaders
are projecting their darkness on the organization and where it
is not safe to bring your spirit and passion.

The leader's responsibility is to make it OK for people to bring their spirit and passion to work with them.

Being enthusiastic about your work doesn't mean you're jumping up and down like a cheerleader, glad-handing, or displaying any hint of insincere behavior. You are *authentic.* When people watch you at work, they know you care deeply about what you do. They know you understand the importance of the work, you understand yourself and the work that needs to be done, and you are persistent in its pursuit. You approach your responsibilities with positive expectations rather than fear. You create a fun and stimulating work environment.

You can't light a fire with a wet match. (Anonymous)

In addition, people watch the leaders of their organization to see if they want to aspire to a leadership role. So, serve as a positive role model who loves the work, and more great leaders will follow in your footsteps.

Being *authentic* also means that what you see is what you get. It may not always be pretty, but it is always real enough to take to the bank. We often see our politicians fall into the trap of following the advice of their poll watchers and professional "handlers." They lose their sense of self in their attempts to curry the support of would-be voters. As soon as that happens, they lose their authenticity and their connection with their followers. School leaders, if not careful, can fall into this very same trap. There is no "one type" of model school leader. The most important thing is to be yourself wherever you go.

I once did a superintendent search for a mid-size district. This district should have been great—it had adequate resources, good people on staff, a supportive community, a decent board. But it was only average in terms of performance. As part of the process, I met with a variety of groups to talk about why candidates would want to come to that district and what characteristics the new superintendent should have. During those sessions, it became apparent that the district felt "flat," and there wasn't a high degree of energy, district pride, or enthusiasm on the part of its people. I learned that the outgoing superintendent was viewed as very competent, but he was fairly introverted and, as the Irish poets Yeats wrote, "had an abiding sense of tragedy which sustained him through temporary periods of joy."

The board ended up selecting a woman who was the exact opposite of this predecessor. She, too, was competent, but she saw all the possibilities in the district, brought energy and enthusiasm to her role, and managed to spread that enthusiasm to the staff and community. Within three years, that district was believing in itself and flying again. Everyone won, because of the impact her positive, authentic and enthusiastic personality had upon the district and the community.

Putting It into Practice

Daily Reflection: On the way into work each day, think about what issues may be on the agenda. How will you meet these challenges—from a positive or negative frame of mind? Will you leave your staff energized by, or disheartened by these challenges? How can you help them develop confidence and enthusiasm for the work?

---

6. Peak Performing School Leaders assume the role of first learner, first teacher, first advocate, and first collaborator on behalf of children.

The First Learner. Remember—you are in a position of responsibility for a learning organization. The school leader has to be a continuous consumer of knowledge—about how to do this work better and be a better leader. If not, no one else in the organization is going to take learning as seriously as employees of a learning organization should.

The First Teacher. Even if you aren't in the classroom, you are still teaching every day—you just have older students. School leaders teach by example. Everything you say and do sends a message. Model great teaching in your work with administrators, teachers, parents, board members, and community leaders. And teach everyone in the organization how to be a great leader—you're going to need all of the great leaders you can grow in order to create a school or system of schools that will meet the needs of every child.

> He who dares to teach must never cease to learn. *(Anonymous)*

Also realize that if you are the superintendent, one of your responsibilities is to help teach your board how to be a great board. Some of the best superintendents I've known pass along pertinent articles in weekly board mailings, use current situations to create "teachable moments," and view their work with the board as coaching. They would never publicly declare that they are the board's coach or teacher, but they quietly assume the responsibility. (Refer to our monograph on Peak Performing Governance Teams for more information on this topic.)

The First Advocate. All of the children who walk through your doors have different levels of voice. By this I mean they have different levels of power and representation—based on who they are, the families they come from, if their parents happen to know a teacher, if they even have parents. All of these factors have an influence on a child's status and voice within the institution. As school leader, you have to assume the role of first advocate for every single child, especially those with little or no voice. The biblical statement of "whatever you do unto the least of these, so also you do unto me" (Matthew 25:40) has direct implications for school leaders. You must assume responsibility and advocacy for the least among us. There will be many times when the interests of adults will be expressed in the loudest and most persistent voice. Some of these interests may be inconsistent with the best interests of all children. *Your job is to advocate for the children first.*

In recent years, a number of superintendents I have worked with have taken on the "sacred cow" of teacher seniority in staff assignments. For decades, common contract language has basically allowed the most senior, and often the best, teachers to choose the easiest teaching assignments—often in the more affluent schools and usually with kids who need their talents the least. The superintendents' objective was to make sure that the students with the greatest needs received the best and most experienced teachers. Not a one who took on this issue did so to the applause of the adults in the system, and not a one escaped without battle scars. But they clearly understood that their job was to advocate for the children first, even when it meant standing alone in the firestorm of adult interests.

The First Collaborator. As school leader, you need to get all the necessary people—other administrators, teachers, board, parents, community leaders—to work together to understand what students need and what must be done to meet those needs. You have to be the first collaborator and assume the role of "Adult" in every relationship. That may mean taking the high road with your most contentious board member or the most challenging union leader.

Being the Adult can mean occasionally setting aside your ego. Recently, the superintendent of a large, urban district attended a board meeting where several community activists—and several board members—were using the opportunity to publicly and personally berate him for recent decisions to close schools and change programs. The decisions were necessary in order to save the district financially and improve the quality of education for children. The board chair never attempted to bring the meeting under control nor tried to maintain a civil atmosphere.

After sitting there and letting people vent for over two hours, the superintendent announced that he was leaving the meeting. His comment to the media was that, "I don't mind the beat-up on me, but it didn't advance anything for the benefit of children." But, he was back at work the next morning, doing what needed to be done, talking with people, and finding fresh ways to advance the educational agenda. You can't let it paralyze you and you can't take it personally.

Building productive relationships will take time, patience, and consistent, humble, persistent effort, but it is a key part of your job as First Collaborator for kids. When school leaders lose their patience and decide that they are going to give up on building a constructive relationship with key constituents, they have begun to mark the conclusion of their tenure in that particular leadership role. **If you can't build the coalitions to support the interests of children, you'll never become the leader the children deserve.**

Putting It into Practice

Think of an initiative you will soon be starting. Read **ASSIGNMENT 5: POLITICAL MAPPING** on page 83 of the *Leadership Work Book* section of this monograph. Complete Steps 1 and 2 of this process, identifying the key constituents you will need to collaborate with for this project to be successful.

---

7. Peak Performing School Leaders are visionary, define success in measurable terms, and have a strategy for achieving success.

Proverbs 29:18 tells us that, "where there is no vision, the people perish." Max De Pree, chairman emeritus of Herman Miller, Inc. and noted author of Leadership is an Art, says the first and most important thing leaders do is articulate a shared vision. Leaders must continually work to define the most ideal future we can conceive for our children and our schools. The vision has to be one that you as the leader can be enthusiastic about—one that you can stand up in front of any group on a moment's notice and articulate clearly and passionately.

The vision must be so clear that it drives the leader's action on a daily basis. The vision also needs to provide a stretch for the organization. People do not get passionate about incremental goals. Johann Wolfgang von Goethe advised leaders to, "Dream no small dreams for they have no power to move the hearts of men." At the same time, the vision must be achievable and believable in the minds of those who will have to do the work to fulfill that vision.

I have a dream…..

(Martin Luther King)

Your vision is your key lever in moving the organization forward because it provides focus for the system. If there is no clearly defined "significantly better place," the organization will languish. The more people within the organization who understand the vision and carry the vision themselves, the less conflict there will be. There will be a greater level of motivation and commitment.

This doesn't mean you create a vision on your own nor have one that isn't shared. But it must be a vision that, in the final analysis, truly "turns you on" professionally. If it doesn't, your would-be followers will tune you out.

Having a vision, however, isn't the only key to success. Having a **clear definition of what success means and establishing metrics around that definition of success** are also critical. A major predictor of failure, whether personal or organizational, is a lack of clarity or definition of success. As one principal says, "If you can't measure it, you'll never master it!" I see far too many schools and systems go through the process of working with the school community to create a shared vision, mission and values, but then do not take that critical next step of establishing clear indicators of success. They are either too undisciplined to create good metrics, or they don't want anyone to ever know they aren't accomplishing what they are supposed to be accomplishing. In other words, they don't want to be held accountable.

A personal example here comes from a well-to-do suburban district with a great reputation and a very popular superintendent. I was facilitating their district-wide planning process. A fifty-member community task force had been established, with all board members and the superintendent involved. It was a great group to work with, and over several weeks we drafted the vision, mission, guiding principles and values, and indicators of success for the district. The next logical and planned step in the process involved a good deal of staff work around establishing measurement instruments, baseline data and specific performance targets.

That's when I got a call from the board president and superintendent, who made their concerns very clear. The district was perceived as an outstanding district by its constituents, and creating a structure that would make them publicly accountable for specific targeted results was a risk they weren't willing to take.

Needless to say, the process concluded diplomatically, the good work of the task force was applauded by the school community, the almost-complete plan was unanimously adopted by the board, and the concept of accountability and transparency in the system became a moot point.

Remember, accountability starts at the top. School leaders have to assume personal and public accountability for the success or failure of the organization in terms that are measurable in both time and accomplishment. If they do not, no one else, including teachers and students, can ever truly be held accountable.

When leaders don't define success, everyone will define it on their own terms; anything anyone does will be OK and everything anyone does will be subject to question and challenge. Most people and most organizations that fail do so in large part because they have not taken the time to step back, clearly define success, and determine how it will be measured.

In too many instances, school leaders defer to the state or federal government for their definition of success. Doing so confuses *compliance* with *success* and, all too often, establishes a bar for kids and adults that is far too low and will never require them to stretch to their potential. For example, under federal law (as of this publication date) each state has the flexibility to establish its own standards. The vast majority of those standards are significantly below what children need to know to compete internationally, but ensure that the state failure rates won't look too bad. Districts need to establish a high bar in terms of additional student metrics—acceptance into and success in college, SAT scores, graduation rates, and more.

Great leaders also have a **strategy** for achieving success—a strategy that connects the ends with the means (with the ends being the vision and the means being the goals and objectives of the organization.) The strategic plan must be a living, breathing document. If one strategy doesn't work, don't continue to pursue the same strategy year after year— or even for a month—hoping for different results. Stop and find out what *does* work. This is part of being tireless and focused. Make changes in direction when you find out that the way you're going isn't getting you where you need to be.

Putting It into Practice

Reflection Exercise: How do you define and measure success for yourself? How do you measure success for your team? Is this clear to your staff and your constituents?

---

8. Peak Performing School Leaders are politically astute.

It's been said that being a school leader is like wrestling a gorilla. You don't stop when you get tired; you stop when the gorilla gets tired. School leaders must be politically astute. Like it or not, this is a public role often surrounded by competing interest groups.

Unfortunately, "politics" has gotten a bad name thanks to the behavior of numerous practitioners in our nation's capital and in state houses around the country. In this context, however, politics should not be viewed as something demeaning or shady. It is how you get things done for kids. We've all seen leaders who have an uncanny ability to create mountains out of mole hills. They're the ones that can't seem to shake problems—everything sticks to them. We call them **"Velcro" leaders**. On the other hand, we've also seen leaders take on the most challenging issues and come through the other end with no lingering baggage. We call them **"Teflon" leaders**. The difference is political acumen.

If you're not at the table, you may be on the menu.
(Phyllis Hunter)

A new superintendent's political skills made an incredible difference in one urban district. This superintendent found himself having to address a huge, looming budget crisis by closing one-third of the district's schools within his first eight months on the job. The district had seen its enrollment decline by half over the past decade, but had never made corresponding adjustments to facilities or staffing. Although new to the role, this superintendent was a former state legislator, and was from a political family, so he knew how to manage issues through a process. He skillfully brought the community along and put the board in the position of voting the school closing package up or down as a whole based upon objective criteria—age and condition of buildings, impact on local community, and past academic performance of the schools. The board could not duck the issue, nor play individual politics with individual schools. And after they voted, the superintendent even gave them the credit and made them feel good for making a courageous decision.

At the other end of the spectrum, I witnessed a superintendent in a small, rural district completely misread the local political landscape. The community's power structure was dominated by three long-standing families, who were well-represented on the board and on the teaching and administrative staff of the district—including one serving as coach of the high school's very successful football team. It didn't take long for the superintendent's ego to feel a little threatened by the coach's power and stature within the community. Upon receiving a parent complaint about the coach, the superintendent called the coach in and told him in no uncertain terms that if he got one more complaint from a parent, the coach would be fired. The coach tried to explain the situation, but the superintendent didn't care to listen.

At the next board meeting, the superintendent was fired, and the elementary principal was appointed as superintendent. (He just happened to be the coach's cousin.)

"Playing politics" from the perspective of the school leader is simply the exercise of common sense and sensitivity to the interests of others in a sometimes highly volatile political environment. It should be viewed as:
-   the discipline of thoughtfully identifying those who will have an interest in your agenda or particular initiative,
-   determining what their interests are and the strength and depth of those interests,
-   determining the significance of their potential for impact on your agenda, then
-   making a strategic decision whether you are going to
    o   engender their support
    o   mitigate their opposition, or

o   selectively ignore them

Herb Kelleher, as CEO of Southwest Airlines, put it best by saying: "Politics has gotten a bad name. But politics really means dealing with people. Being political is something everybody should be because it means learning what motivates people, what concerns people, what scares people, what inspires people in order to have them act affirmatively and effectively."

Being politically astute also involves flexibility. You should have a clear vision of the outcome, but maintain flexibility about how you get there. Understand what people need and see if their concerns can be addressed as you move toward the goal.

> *If you're doing something significant with your life, you have to be attacked. It's required.*
> *(Ruth Simmons)*

One tool I've used to help develop political acumen is well-established practice of "Political Mapping." This tool should be used when entering a new leadership position, or starting a new initiative. It provides a disciplined way to overcome our limited ability to just do this intuitively. Refer to Assignment 5: Political Mapping in the Leadership Work Book section of this monograph.

Putting It into Practice

Think of an initiative you will be starting soon. Complete **ASSIGNMENT 5: POLITICAL MAPPING** on page 83 of the *Leadership Workbook* section of this monograph. This will help you think through the political implications of this project and how you will plan to address them.

---

9. *Peak Performing School Leaders are trustworthy and competent.*

Every one of us longs for autonomy in our lives—having autonomy is critical to being able to meet our own psychological needs. We don't meet our needs in a way prescribed by someone else. The prescription has to be our own—based upon our values, beliefs, and personal indicators of success. As a school leader, if you are going to be free to pursue your goals, you must have a certain degree of autonomy.

However, it is important to remember that as a school leader, autonomy can be taken away from you by those above you or by those below you in the organization. People will not allow you to exercise autonomy if they don't believe you are both *trustworthy* and *competent*. They must feel they can trust you, and they must believe you know what you're doing.

The building of trust takes time, particularly where trust has been lacking. It also takes continuous effort and focus on the part of the leader. If leadership is all about relationships, relationships are all about trust. Keep in mind that almost everything leaders say and do has the potential to either build or destroy trust. Covey says that every interaction with another person either makes a deposit in, or a withdrawal from, their emotional bank account. Make sure that building trust (making deposits) is a cornerstone of your leadership practice.

Creating the environment and structures for provision of honest feedback to you as a leader is critical to establishing trust. Leaders must have a willingness to be transparent, open and honest, and to accept feedback or criticism without recrimination. Many school leaders say they have an "open door policy." But as one superintendent says, just having an open door isn't good enough. You also have to have an open mind and an open heart.

Some school leaders are starting to use a tool common in the private sector—the 360 degree feedback tool. Receiving feedback in this way can be helpful in the identification and elimination of personal blind spots.

The point is to not just create the opportunities for random feedback, but to make it part of who you are and how you grow as a leader.

A former principal shared one of his first lessons on leadership and trust. He was in his first year as a principal in a small rural community. The district had a very successful band director whose students had won numerous competitions and awards and were considered, over the years, to be one of the best small school bands in the state. The director had a reputation of being very no-nonsense in practice. She knew her vision, mission, and beliefs. One day this young principal went to the practice room to watch and observe the director. He saw the intensity, the demanding voice, all the organization and structure. The band was working on a new composition with very limited success. She was pushing the group to keep playing one passage, over and over, but something was just not clicking. Finally, one of the students yelled, "Time out!" and proceeded to explain to the director why the passage was not working. The director asked some questions and said to the young musician, "You're right!" Adjustments were made and the piece worked. This teacher was a leader. Yes, she was tough, knew her vision and what she wanted, but she also had trust and respect and openness with her musicians, allowing them to speak up and give an opinion.

Covey also has another saying about building trust. He reminds us, "If you want the loyalty of those who are present, be loyal to those who are absent." Leaders cannot engage in talking about people to other people. That does not demonstrate loyalty and makes people wonder what you are saying about them behind their backs.

The other necessary ingredient of this characteristic of Peak Performing School Leadership is competence. *Competence* is a combination of native intellect, pertinent knowledge, relevant skills, capacity to execute, and a persistent and humble attitude of learning towards your work.

Many state and national associations, universities and accrediting bodies have identified the technical competencies for school leadership. *The Interstate School Leaders Licensure Consortium Standards for School Leaders* is one example of this. It is not the purpose of this monograph to discuss the technical competencies of school leadership in detail. But school leaders must continually assess their technical competencies and continually work to enhance their personal competency as a leader.

Putting It into Practice

Reflection Exercise: In my role, what actions can I take to build and strengthen trust with my key constituents? What have I observed other leaders do to destroy trust? What specific school leadership competencies do I need to strengthen?

---

10. Peak Performing School Leaders have the courage to "lead deep."

Finally, strong leadership means having the courage to **lead deep**—to live your values, your beliefs, your knowledge, and your truth—and not waver from those guide posts. At times, simply due to "politics," you may need to time the execution of certain strategies. You can't do everything at once. I've seen some leaders develop very ambitious agendas that are completely justified and absolutely needed—but scared their followers and constituent groups to the point of inaction or outright resistance.

While your agenda must be thoughtful, measured, and politically sensitive, you must be continually moving forward—for the benefit of children and for your own peace of mind and soul.

So many times I see leaders who do not fully know themselves or what they believe, and therefore do not have the courage to do what should be done—making tough decisions, firing someone who needs to be fired. They simply go along to get along. The organization drifts with little clarity or coherence.

> *The truth of the matter is that you always know the right thing to do. The hard part is doing it.*
> *(Norman Schwarzkopf)*

As Shakespeare wrote, "A coward dies a thousand deaths, a hero only one." *(Julius Caesar)* Great leaders have the courage to do what needs to be done at the deepest levels to make sure every child gets the best education possible.

Once, while observing a candidate interview for a superintendency, the board asked the candidate what the most difficult professional decision was that he ever had to make. The candidate's eyes went to the ceiling and there was a long pause. Then he responded, "The decision to fire my very best, lifelong friend." With some emotion he went on to explain that he had been instrumental, with full disclosure, in his friend's employment with the district. But over time, his friend, to his dismay, ignored the well-being of children through his words and deeds, and then disregarded initial requests and admonishments to change his behavior. It came down to the choice between his belief system about the interests of kids, or his best friend's job.

That's having the courage to lead deep.

As I mentioned in the introduction to this monograph, over the past dozen years I've had an incredibly rich opportunity to work with aspiring and established leaders from all walks of life as they've taken on school leadership roles at all levels across the country. I firmly believe that "school people" are some of the best people on the face of the earth. Many of these people have been good, solid leaders—some even great leaders.

A few of these leaders stand out in my mind as having had the courage to lead deep. I hesitate to single out one example. But these are the special leaders who are clear about what they believe, know who they are and why they were put here, and have a clear and compelling vision for children. They see what needs to be done, and they figure out a way to get it done—time after time. These leaders have mastered all of the other nine characteristics of peak performing leadership and have added the ingredient of courage to make them great.

Putting It into Practice

Reflection Exercise: What difficult decision am I struggling with where I know the right thing to do, but need an extra dose of courage in order to do it?

Concluding Thoughts on Leadership

Great leaders are great people, and it begins with who they are as individuals. "Incomplete" people are never great leaders, except perhaps for a fleeting moment in time. They may be able to lead in a short-term crisis situation, but over an extended period of time can never become enduring, peak performing leaders.

Often times I see people attain apparent success without demonstrating many of these Characteristics of Peak Performing School Leaders. They may have assumed their leadership roles for the wrong reasons. They may treat people poorly. They may be shameless self-promoters. Following a discussion of these Characteristics of Peak Performing School Leaders, I'm often asked, "What about the people who are surviving and even appear to be thriving in leadership roles, but who are not great—or even good—people?" History is replete with glaring examples.

I have discovered in life that there are ways of getting almost anywhere you want to go, if you really want to go.
(Langston Hughes)

The best answer I've found to this question comes from the legendary Green Bay Packer Coach Vince Lombardi, who said that, "Any person who leads for any purpose other than the common good of his followers sows the seeds of self-destruction in his path." In other words, if you watch the careers of incomplete people in leadership roles for a long enough period of time, they will eventually self-destruct. They may reach retirement, but may not be able to point to a single situation where they left their world a better place.

Conversely, the legacy of a Peak Performing School Leader may not be immediately known. Good people and great leaders may end up being fired by an unwitting board or supervisor for all kinds of wrong reasons unrelated to the quality of their leadership.

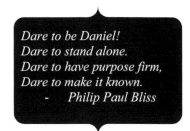

Dare to be Daniel!
Dare to stand alone.
Dare to have purpose firm,
Dare to make it known.
-   Philip Paul Bliss

Peak Performing School Leaders are unafraid of this. They will know that **they** did not fail—the situation failed them. They will know in their hearts that they did the best they could for children and that their legacy will remain forever in the hearts and minds of their followers. Their place will never be with "those cold and timid souls who know neither victory nor defeat."

Finally, keep in mind that life and leadership are both inextricably intertwined. Both are a homeward journey, and both need your continued focus and best efforts.

Good luck on your leadership journey.

PUTTING PEAK PERFORMING SCHOOL LEADERSHIP INTO PRACTICE:

LEADERSHIP WORK BOOK

ASSIGNMENT 1: DEFINING LEADERSHIP

Anyone assuming a leadership role ought to have a working definition of what leadership is all about, from their own perspective. This is important not only for framing their own work, but also for helping other would-be leaders within the organization understand and develop their own capacities. This exercise is designed to help you draft your own personal definition of leadership.

Step One: Identify the three greatest leaders you have known personally through observation, or through your readings. Define the qualities, characteristics or skills that put them on your Top 3 list.

Leader 1 _____

    Qualities, Characteristics, Skills:
        a.

        b.

        c.

        d.

        e.

Leader 2 _____

    Qualities, Characteristics, Skills:
        a.

        b.

        c.

        d.

        e.

Leader 3 _____

    Qualities, Characteristics, Skills:
      a.

      b.

      c.

      d.

      e.

Step Two: Based upon your observations, readings, and personal experiences, draft your personal definition of leadership.

Step Three: Now, reduce this definition to one clear, concise, and coherent statement.

Remember that leadership is complex, and how you define it will evolve over time as you grow as a leader. Take the time every two or three years to reflect and update your definition so it is consistent with your current values, knowledge, and beliefs.

ASSIGNMENT 2: PERSONAL LEADERSHIP PLAN

Do not think about entering a leadership role before you have really thought through your personal leadership plan, which is a tool for achieving self-mastery. Take time to revisit and update this plan each year. (The basis of this planning is loosely adapted from concepts presented in Stephen Covey's The Seven Habits of Highly Effective People.)

Step 1. Think prospectively about your contributions and accomplishments—what you want to do. Answer the following questions:

a.   When I look at my work life, which activities do I consider of greatest worth?

b.   When I look at my personal life, which activities do I consider of greatest worth?

c.   What talents and skills do I have?

d. What do I consider to be my most important future contribution to others?

e. If I had unlimited time and resources, what would I want to do?

Step 2. Make a list of all the things you want <u>to have</u> that you feel are important. Your "haves" may be tangible possessions (e.g. a vacation home) or they may be intangible (e.g. a strong, happy family). It may be helpful to create two lists—one for your personal life and one for your professional life. Identify the five most important items in each area.

    Personal Life:
    1.

    2.

    3.

    4.

    5.

Professional Life:
   1.

   2.

   3.

   4.

   5.

Step 3. People influence others through their behavior, feelings, and lifestyle. Thinking about people who have influenced you will help you discover the character traits you value most.

a.   List the people who have served as positive role models or mentors for you and have had a significant impact on your life. In what way did they influence you?

b.   What qualities do these people possess that I would like to emulate?

c.   What other *qualities of character* do I most admire in others?

d.   Therefore, what *values and principles* will guide my
        life and my leadership?

**Step 4: In your personal and work life, you may act in
several roles. You may be a spouse, a parent, an
administrator, a volunteer, a friend.**

a.   Identify up to five critical roles you assume.

        1.

        2.

        3.

        4.

        5.

b.   Next, visualize your retirement celebration. All the key
     people from each of your roles are attending and paying
     tribute. For each role, write a brief statement describing
     what tribute you would hope they give you, and how
     they would describe you.

        Role 1:

Role 2:

Role 3:

Role 4:

Role 5:

c. Identify your ultimate **goal** for each **role** and how you
   will know you have achieved it. What strategies will
   help you achieve each goal?

Role	Ultimate Goal	How Will I Know I've Achieved It?	Strategies for Success/Next Steps
1.			
2.			
3.			
4.			
5.			

Step 5: Now, draft your statements of mission and vision.

What is my purpose in this world?

What is my vision for myself five years into the future? Ten years? Twenty years?

Step 6: Putting it into practice. Leaders must care for themselves and continually improve in the four major areas of their life:

> ➤ Physical health
> ➤ Intellectual growth
> ➤ Social/emotional relationships
> ➤ Spiritual health

For each of the four areas, identify your personal goals and how you will know you are achieving them. What can you do to start achieving the goals? Revisit this action plan *each week* and put items on your calendar that will help you move closer toward your goals.

Area: Physical Health

    Goal:

    Indicators of Success:

    Action Steps:

Area: Intellectual Growth

    Goal:

    Indicators of Success:

    Action Steps:

Area: Social/Emotional Relationships

Goal:

Indicators of Success:

Action Steps:

Area: Spiritual Health

Goal:

Indicators of Success:

Action Steps:

ASSIGNMENT 3: STATEMENTS OF BELIEF

School leaders must be able to clearly articulate their beliefs about the various members of the school community— *beliefs about their potential and their role in developing children.* These beliefs become a basis for the three stories that leaders must be able to tell: First, they must tell their own story—who they are, key learnings, and experiences that brought them to this point in their leadership journey. Second, leaders must be able to tell the story of the organization they lead—past, present and future. And third, they must tell the story of the followers to help them visualize their role in that future. Think through your beliefs and convert them to "talking points." See example statements in Appendix A for starter ideas.

What do you believe about **children and their capacity to achieve**?

What do you believe about **the role of schools**?

What do you believe about **leadership teams**?

What do you believe about **the role of principals**?

What do you believe about **effective governance**?

What do you believe about **the role of teachers**?

What do you believe about **the role of parents**?

What do you believe about **the role of the community in supporting its children**?

ASSIGNMENT 4: YOUR LEADERSHIP STORY

What is a Leadership Story?

Leaders must be able to tell their story in a succinct and compelling fashion to a variety of audiences. This story will help followers understand who you are, why you are here, and why they should follow you.

Key Components of Your Leadership Story: Themes that should run throughout your story

Your core values
What are you most passionate about in life and why? What values drive your interactions with others and your work? How have the values of the people in your life influenced you? These core values should connect to a theme that runs throughout and links to your introduction, history, and professional experiences.

Your leadership strengths
Don't be afraid to "toot your own horn" here. If it is done appropriately within the context of the rest of the story, you can deliver this message without being boastful or overly arrogant. Your strengths can also be a theme that runs throughout and links to your introduction, history, and professional experiences.

Significant other people
These are the people that you loved, liked, or respected to the extent that you were willing to change the course of your life for them. Share how they influenced you at key points in your life.

Turning points/"ah-ha" moments
In sharing your personal history and professional experiences, highlight key turning points or pivotal

experiences that significantly changed how you saw yourself or where you wanted to go.

Telling Your Story

Timing
The telling of your story should ideally take 10 minutes, 15 minutes maximum. If the story is too long, you may lose the interest of your audience. Too short and you don't have time to explore all of the important story elements.

Presentation style
Your story should not be told with power point slides—you should be speaking from your heart.

Potential Leadership Story Outline

Leadership stories should be personalized, so feel free to use a different structure than the outline below if it makes more sense for your story.

Engaging introduction
Begin with a quote, story, anecdote, or similar attention-grabbing way to engage the audience and introduce a "theme" that runs throughout your story (see key components above). This gives the audience an idea of who you are without giving away the story, and creates anticipation.

Your history
Share critical experiences and people that shaped your core beliefs and personal characteristics. This should be personal, engaging, memorable, heartfelt and/or humorous. Stories and examples of growing up should not just be isolated events, but should be tied together with some type of structure to help the audience understand how it all ties together and

contributes to who you are today, and in particular, what leadership traits you learned.

Your professional experiences
These should include the key job experiences, mentors, and lessons learned that shaped your core values, career goals, and leadership strengths today. Pivotal experiences are more important than comprehensiveness.

Your job today and/or your future dreams
What does all of this mean for you? In what ways can you best contribute to the world? Where do you want to go with your life? Why does being here, now, make sense for you and fit into your "calling?" What would make you most proud in the future?

Conclusion
Wrap up with something that elegantly summarizes what you want your audience to remember most about you. Your audience will most frequently remember your introduction and conclusion more than any other part of your story. Make this clear, strong, and well-planned.

ASSIGNMENT 5: POLITICAL MAPPING

Political Mapping is a process for developing political acumen. Creating a political map can help overcome our limited capacity as humans to simply do this intuitively. Inviting the participation of all leadership team members in this process can also help develop their abilities to think strategically, plus gain their ownership in project success. The political mapping process is often taught in many business schools, but is rarely presented in graduate schools of education.

As a new leader, you need to create a political map to:
- identify all the individuals and groups that will potentially play a role in your success—or failure
- identify the *primary* community influencers and those who influence them
- determine how you will get to know them and understand their interests

When beginning a new initiative, it is important to create a political map to:
- identify all those who are likely to have an interest in the change or proposal being initiated
- identify the *primary* influencers and those who influence them
- determine which of those groups or individuals
  - o need to be approached for support
  - o need to have their concerns mitigated
  - o will have charges to defend against
  - o should simply be ignored

Steps in the Mapping Process

The basic process for political mapping is as follows.
1. Clearly state the change or initiative to be undertaken and place that statement in a circle.
2. Begin to identify, in satellite fashion, each of the people or groups who are likely to have an interest in

the change. There are likely to be 5-15 satellites. The bigger the initiative, the more satellites there will be.

3. For each satellite created, determine whether this individual/group is likely to be supportive, adverse, or neutral regarding the proposed change or initiative.
4. For each satellite created, determine if the potential impact of this person or group is High, Medium, or Low.
5. For all High and Medium impact satellites, create a new set of satellites, indicating the specific individuals or groups who need to be contacted. There may be approximately 15-45 sub-satellites here.
6. For each individual or group who needs to be contacted, create an assignment chart, listing strategies, talking points, time lines, and persons responsible for the intervention.

Assignment

Think of a change or initiative you will soon be implementing. Complete the political mapping process for this change, either on your own or with your leadership team. You may use the following worksheets to help you get started.

Political Mapping Diagram Worksheet

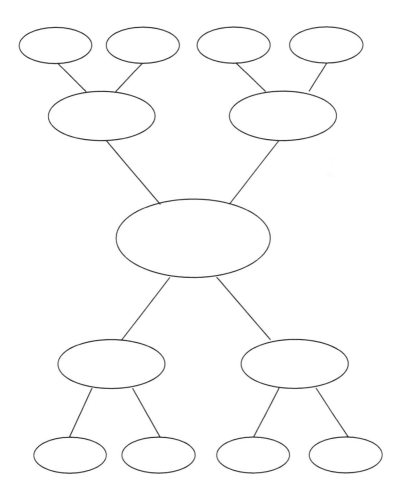

Political Mapping Assignment Chart Worksheet

Influencer	Strategy	Person Responsible	Time Line

APPENDIX A: SAMPLE STATEMENTS OF BELIEF

Following are example statements of belief regarding the role and expectations of each of the players in an education system. Use these ideas as a springboard to create your own complete set of beliefs.

Beliefs about children and their capacity to achieve:

- All children have the capacity to learn at the highest levels of our curriculum, if we have the capacity to teach them.
- The human genome project has shown us that all people are 99.9% genetically identical, regardless of race, gender, and ethnicity.
-
-

Beliefs about teachers:

- We are at our best as human beings when we are growing or helping others grow.
- Teaching is one of the most important, challenging and potentially rewarding roles in the world.
- Every teacher has the opportunity to stand out in the lives of tomorrow's adults as one of the 5-7 most significant people who have influenced their lives.
- Great teachers are great human beings and great leaders.
-
-

Beliefs about the role of parents:

- Parents are the first and most important teachers in the lives of their children.

- A parent's actions are a child's most important lessons.
- Parents are the first partners of teachers and schools in the education of children.
-
-

Beliefs about the role of principals:

- Principals are the first learners and first teachers within their buildings.
- Principals must have the highest expectations for themselves, their teachers, and the children for whom they are responsible.
- Principals must have the courage to hold themselves publicly and personally accountable for providing the highest quality education of children in their buildings.
-
-

Beliefs about the role of the community in supporting its children:

Communities that create and support school systems have a responsibility to ensure the success of the schools by:
- Electing quality individuals to govern the schools
- Making sure that the system has a clear definition of success around student learning and has established a corresponding system of accountability
- Providing support systems which go beyond the capacity of the schools to meet the needs of all children
- Prioritizing the needs of children in every community decision
-
-

Beliefs about school governance:

- Peak performing governance teams establish clear indicators of success for the district.
- Chaos in the board room will result in chaos in the classroom.
- Board members must come to their role with one pure motive—service to all the children of the district.
-
-

APPENDIX B: BOOK STUDY DISCUSSION

Many school leaders have book study clubs with their teams. If you are using this monograph in your book club, here are some starter discussion questions for the group. These questions could also be used in a leadership team retreat.

- How have you defined leadership? What is your definition of leadership?

- Do you believe that educators, as a whole, feel that their calling is related to their work, rather than related to an avocation? Do you think this is *more true/ as true as/ less true* than in other professions?

- Share one of your belief statements. How does holding this belief impact your work?

- What are some strategies you can use to maintain balance in your life, and be successful in implementing your personal leadership plan?

- What are visible ways you can communicate enthusiasm and spirit in your daily work?

- How do you define success with your team? How is it measured, and is your team performance transparent?

- What difficult decisions are you struggling with where you know the right thing to do, but would need an extra dose of courage in order to do it?

- What was your biggest take-away from this book?

- What do you plan to do differently in your work as a leader as a result of reading this book?

APPENDIX C: FURTHER SUGGESTED READINGS ON LEADERSHIP

There are currently over 50,000 books on the topic of leadership available. Here are the books and articles that have most shaped my thinking. Some are classics in the field, some are biographies of great leaders, and others are simply well worth your time.

"Building the Bridge as You Walk on It," Robert Quinn, *Leader to Leader*, Fall 2004.

"Crucibles of Leadership," Warren Bennis and Robert Thomas, Harvard Business School Publishing Corporation, 2002.

Developing the Leader Within You, John C. Maxwell, Thomas Nelson Publishers, 2005.

Do You! 12 Laws to Access the Power in You to Achieve Happiness and Success, Russell Simmons, Gotham, 2007.

A Game Plan for Life: The Power of Mentoring, John Wooden, Bloomsbury, 2009.

Good to Great, Jim Collins, HarperBusiness, 2001.

Good to Great and the Social Sectors, Jim Collins, HarperBusiness, 2005.

Handbook of Leadership Development, Center for Creative Leadership, McCauley, Moxley, Van Velsor, Editors, Jossey-Bass, 1998.

Insights on Leadership: Service, Stewardship, Spirit, and Servant-Leadership, Larry Spears, Editor, John Wiley & sons, Inc., 1998.

Jack: Straight from the Gut, Jack Welch, Warner Books, 2001.

Lead, Follow, Or Get Out Of the Way, Robert D. Ramsey, Corwin Press, 2005.

Leadership, Rudolph W. Giuliani, Hyperion, 2002.

Leadership: Enhancing the Lessons of Experience, Hughes, Ginnett, Curphy, Irwin, 1996.

Leadership and the New Science: Discovering Order in a Chaotic World, Margaret Wheatley, Berrett-Koehler Publishers, 2006.

Leading Minds: An Anatomy of Leadership, Howard Gardner, BasicBooks, 1995.

Leading With Soul, Lee Bolman and Terrence Deal, Jossey-Bass, 2001.

Learning to Lead: A Workbook on Becoming a Leader, Warren Bennis, Joan Goldsmith, Perseus Books, 1997.

Let Your Life Speak: Listening for the Voice of Vocation, Parker J. Palmer, Jossey-Bass, 2000.

"Level 5 Leadership: The Triumph of Humility and Fierce Resolve," Jim Collins, *Harvard Business Review*, January 2001.

Lincoln On Leadership, Donald T. Phillips, Warner Books, Inc., 1993.

My American Journey, Colin Powell, Random House, 1995.

On Becoming a Servant Leader, Robert K. Greenleaf, Jossey-Bass Publishers, 1996. (essays written 1959-1969).

"Practicing Servant-Leadership," Larry Spears, *Leader to Leader*, Fall 2004.

Principle-Centered Leadership, Stephen Covey, Simon & Shuster, 1991.

The Change Masters, Rosabeth Moss Kanter, Free Press, 1985.

The Courage to Teach: Exploring the Inner Landscape of a Teacher's Life, Parker Palmer, Jossey-Bass, 2007.

"The Curse of the Superstar CEO," Rakesh Khurana, Harvard Business School Publishing Corporation, 2002.

The Leadership Challenge, James Kouzes, Barry Posner, Jossey-Bass, 1995.

The Leadership Engine: How Winning Companies Build Leaders at Every Level, Noel Tichy, HarperBusiness, 1997.

The Learning Leader: How to Focus School Improvement for Better Results, Douglas Reeves, ASCD 2006.

"The Making of a Corporate Athlete," Jim Loehr and Tony Schwartz, Harvard Business School Publishing Corporation, 2001.

The Seven Habits of Highly Effective People, Stephen Covey, Simon & Schuster, 1989.

Victory in Our Schools, Major General John Stanford, Bantam Books, 1999.

"What's Your Story?" Herminia Ibarra and Kent Lineback, Harvard Business Review, January 2005.

Wooden on Leadership, John Wooden and Steve Jamison, McGraw-Hill, 2005.

About the Authors

Timothy Quinn

Dr. Timothy G. Quinn's career spans teaching and leadership at all levels of public education from K-12 through community college and university. He served as an English teacher, assistant principal, and principal in Michigan, prior to becoming superintendent of the Green Bay Public Schools and serving a term as Wisconsin's Deputy State Superintendent of Instruction. He also served as president of Northwestern Michigan College in Traverse City, Michigan. Dr. Quinn was then appointed by The University of Michigan as chief executive officer of Michigan's first virtual college.

Tim was the founder and former president of the highly successful Michigan Leadership Institute, which is dedicated to leadership development, placement of outstanding leaders, and continuous research on the topic of leadership. As a result of the Institute's work, Tim was engaged by The Eli and Edythe Broad Foundation to partner on the creation of The Broad Center for the Management of School Systems and the Broad Superintendents Academy.

Having been raised on a hog farm in an Irish family with 10 kids, Tim's first leadership position came when he was just seven years old—when his father appointed him Director of Manure Management. He is now a farmer once again, in northern Michigan, and is the proud father of a teacher/coach and a school social worker, with five grandchildren.

Tim earned a Ph.D. in educational leadership from The University of Michigan, and received honorary doctoral degrees for his statewide leadership from Eastern Michigan, Central Michigan and Grand Valley State Universities.

Michelle (Shelley) Keith

Michelle E. Keith's career includes twenty years of higher education experience in the areas of human resources, planning and governance. As a human resources administrator at Iowa State University and as the Director of Human Resources at Northwestern Michigan College, she has had extensive experience in recruitment, employment, and professional development.

Shelley was the co-founder and former vice president of the Michigan Leadership Institute, and was engaged by The Eli and Edythe Broad Foundation to partner on the creation and management of the Broad Superintendents Academy.

She has a bachelor's degree and master's degree from Iowa State University.

Shelley now lives on a farm in northern Michigan with Tim, her life partner, and enjoys gardening, writing, and taking care of all the animals—human and otherwise.

The authors are available for selective consultation, career and executive coaching, and public speaking on leadership, governance and the superintendency. They are most easily reached at:
timquinn@mileader.com
keith@mileader.com

12498011R00056

Made in the USA
Lexington, KY
15 December 2011